I love you because...

The C. R. Gibson Company
Norwalk, Connecticut

I love you because ...

Of all the sentences ever begun, that one must be the hardest to complete. And it must have always been that way, because people have been thinking about love ... writing about love ... trying to add the perfect ending to, "I love you because ... " ever since the world began.

But no one has ever found just the right words to explain ... why one person loves another.

I love you because ...

Lately I've been trying to finish that sentence myself. And in searching for just the right words to show the feelings in my heart, I never quite make it.

Plato once wrote: "At the very touch of love every one becomes a poet."

Before I met you, that idea might not have meant anything to me. But now its beautiful meaning is becoming clear. Of course I'm not really a poet, but I'm beginning to understand what the great writers were talking about when they spoke of love.

With their help, I'll begin to tell you what I've wanted to for so long—why I love you so very much.

This is the true measure of love,
When we believe that we alone can love,
That no one could ever have loved so before us.
And that no one will ever love
In the same way after us.

JOHANN VON GOETHE

That's the way I feel about us. And I like it! It makes me feel very special, unique—knowing that there has never been another couple quite like us.

For someone who has never been in love, this idea might be difficult to understand. It might even seem foolish and egotistical.

But I know and you know. We know that what we share is a one-of-a-kind sort of love.

Everyone who has loved has probably felt some of the things we are feeling now. Still, our love is unique. It makes me think of snowflakes. To someone who glances out a window at a snowstorm, they are all the same. But to someone who looks very closely, it is clear that every snowflake is a masterpiece with a beauty all its own. Never seen before. Never to be seen again. Like the moments of our love.

When we go out together, I can feel others looking at us with wonder, surprise and sometimes a smile reflecting our joy. They can tell that what we share is like nothing else in the world.

People seem to know we're in love the instant they see us. The checker at the market. The man at the filling station. People we pass on the street and never see again. They know and they are glad for us. It must be true that all the world loves a lover.

What we have is too big to keep a secret. It just naturally spills out wherever we go. And this pleases me because I have found that our happiness is increased by sharing.

Love like ours isn't meant to be hoarded, measured out in bits and pieces. We couldn't do that even if we wanted to because love is a living thing with a life and a will of its own.

We can afford to be generous because the more love we give away, the more is returned to us.

It's true, you see. There has never been a couple quite like us. There has never been a love quite like ours. And no one will ever love in the same way after us.

I t's all I have to bring today,
This and my heart beside,
This, and my heart, and all the fields,
And all the meadows wide.

EMILY DICKINSON

Sometimes I'd like to be very rich—to give you the most beautiful presents that money can buy.

It would be nice. But it isn't necessary. I know because of what you have given me—yourself, your love. Gifts like these are beyond price tags, much more wonderful than wealth.

And when you do give me something, no matter what—a four-leaf clover you found on the way to my place, a shell from the beach, a well-thumbed book you want to share—I feel truly "gifted" because of all the love you bring along with your presents.

Since we have come together, I see that there is so much we can give to each other simply by sharing the world around us.

Paul Engle said it this way—
> Because we do
>> All things together
> All things improve,
>> Even weather.
> Our daily meat
>> And bread taste better.
> Trees are greener.
>> Rain is wetter.

That's just the beginning of a very long list of everyday things that have become richer, sharper, more vivid because of experiencing them with you.

It makes me feel like a little child again, seeing beautiful things for the first time, smelling wonderful, exciting aromas. Even a hamburger can be a taste adventure when you're there, across the table from me.

I like the simple times when we're together. Maybe lying on our backs, looking up at the clouds. Not saying much but communicating a lot.

And I like it when we watch old movies on TV. The times when we can't stop laughing. The times in the sad movies when we're very quiet and I look around and see by your eyes that you're feeling the story along with me.

You make small, ordinary things larger than life, extraordinary. And you make the great works of nature sweep across a wider canvas in my mind.

I had almost forgotten about the stars. Now, looking at them with you, they are incredibly bright, indescribably beautiful.

The changing seasons are suddenly more miraculous and exhilarating because we are watching their progress together.

Because we love, this old world is new again and it belongs to us ... and all the fields ... and all the meadows wide.

Love is no hot house flower, but a wild plant, born of a wet night, born of an hour of sunshine, sprung from a wild seed, blown along the road by a wild wind.

JOHN GALSWORTHY

What a wonderful thought. It reminds me of two very special qualities of the love we share—independence and strength.

A long time ago—before you—I used to dream of what it would be like to be in love. I had a lot of ideas about how to make that dream come true.

Foolishly, I thought that by planning, improving myself, working at it, being at the right place at the right time, I could make love happen.

It seemed as simple as growing a plant on my window sill. All you need is the right seed, some soil, a pot, light, water and a little patience. Then you wake up some morning and—Surprise! There she grows!

But love doesn't work like that. You can't make love happen.

Kahlil Gibran said—
Think not that you can direct the course of love, for love, if it finds you worthy, directs your course.

If everyone could simply decide to be in love, then that's exactly where almost everyone would be. Because, after all, it is the most important thing in the world—to love someone who loves you in return.

But love isn't like a hot house flower. It is a wild plant that springs up unplanned and untended. Not fragile, but almost fierce in its will to survive. Not timid, shy, but bold, aggressive and determined to flourish. Not weak, but strong.

I could never explain why I love anybody or anything.

WALT WHITMAN

Why do I love you? For a thousand reasons and then for a thousand more that I'm not even aware of.

I love you because of the way you look, the way your laughter sounds, the special way you walk and talk and hold me.

I love you because of your beliefs and your ambitions. For where you've been and what you are becoming.

I love your strengths and your weaknesses, the times when you're serious or silly ... all the different "you's" that go together to make YOU.

But that doesn't even begin to tell you. Your whole is somehow more than the sum of your parts. And all the love I feel for you is greater than all the reasons that I know for loving.

I can never tell you all the "because's" but I want to keep trying. There'll be a lot of time for that in the months and years ahead of us.

Just please remember that explaining a miracle is never quick or easy.

It is strange that people will talk of miracles, revelations, inspirations, and the like, as things past, while love remains.

HENRY DAVID THOREAU

I do believe that love is a miracle. Especially our love. The dictionary says that a miracle is:

> *(1) an extraordinary event manifesting a supernatural work of God*
>
> *(2) an extremely outstanding or unusual event, thing or accomplishment.*

That sounds like love to me.

Some might say that love can't compare to all the miracles of the ancient world that have mystified people for centuries. But I think love is an even greater mystery than these. Because love didn't happen just a few times in the distant past. It's an ongoing miracle that has touched and changed people's lives since the beginning of time. And it's still going on today, mysteriously and miraculously.

None of our senses can know it but all of our senses respond to it. It is nowhere in particular and everywhere in general at the same time.

Scientists can't explain it. Philosophers can't make much sense of it. Inventors can't create it.

Wars have been fought over it and peace has come out of it.

It is puzzling, impractical, priceless, humble, power-ful, silent, enormous, invisible, ageless, earthshaking, the "every only thing," a miracle—our love.

Love does not consist in gazing at each other, but in looking together in the same direction.

ANTOINE DE SAINT-EXUPÉRY

I'll have to admit that simply looking at you is one of my favorite things. I love seeing you in all your different moods, by sun and candlelight. And if we have to be apart for a few days, I look at your picture over and over again. Then I look at all the pictures of you that are stored up in my mind.

But Mr. de Saint-Exupéry is right. Looking at you isn't nearly as important to me as the times when we are both looking together in the same direction.

Best of all are the times when we look back at where we've been, long before we met each other. And when we look ahead to all that may be waiting for us in the future.

Looking back in time with you, I love hearing about all the things that happened to you along the way of growing up. Good times, bad times. And it's so nice telling you about all the things in my yesterdays that helped me and hurt me. It means a lot knowing that you want to find out about the people and places that made me "me."

We have so many plans, such marvelous dreams. I love those journeys into the future with you, thinking of all the adventures we may have, the places we may go, the discoveries we may find just around the next bend in the road.

Maybe some of our dreams will never come true. We'll take it one day at a time and see.

Regardless, we are looking together in the same direction and sometimes I feel that, clear day or not, we really can see forever.

A crowd is not a company
and faces are but a gallery of pictures,
and talk but a tinkling cymbal,
where there is no love.

FRANCIS BACON

Before you, before love, I never knew what was missing. But I knew I was missing something.

It seemed as if everyone else had some secret, some vital piece of information about life, that I didn't understand, maybe could never know.

Life was nice but a lot of times I would ask myself, "What's the point? Does this really mean anything?" But I couldn't answer those questions for myself and no one else could answer them for me.

It was like living in a kind of fog where nothing was ever really clear.

I went to the right parties and places—where the fun was supposed to be. But it wasn't there for me.

There were all those stories, books, movies that other people felt so deeply. But they never quite reached me.

e. e. cummings knew what the trouble was. He said,

unless you love someone
nothing else makes any sense.

It didn't to me. Not for a long time.

And then came you.

All of a sudden I knew. Exactly what I knew, I can't say in so many words, even today, but I knew I knew.

Before it was like trying to work a very complicated jigsaw puzzle while wearing a blindfold. Occasionally a few of the pieces fit, but nothing ever really came together.

Then you came along and took that blindfold away. And everything that used to seem so confusing became clear.

> . . . today at last
> A letter came,
> One tiny, narrow sheet.
>
> Tonight I've lit my lamp
> A hundred times
> To read its words of love.
>
> LIN I NING
> CH'ING DYNASTY

These words, written so many centuries ago, have special meaning for me today.

You'd be surprised to know what it means to me when I get a letter from you or a note or a card. There's something about seeing the way you feel in writing. Perhaps because there's a permanency about it.

I do save those pieces of paper that bring me your words. I read them over and over, long after they've been committed to memory, until the creases start to tear from many openings and closings.

They are part of the souvenirs that I keep to remind me of us. And there are so many more. Ticket stubs from plays we enjoyed together, match covers from restaurants where we have lingered over coffee until the waiter started looking at his watch and giving us the eye, crazy doodles of yours that I've found by the phone.

On the open market all these bits and pieces that I have stored away would be worth exactly nothing. But to me they are very precious because I can get them out and sort through them every once in a while ... and know that what seems too good to be true isn't a dream.

They are proof. Love is. We are.

*A*nd this is love: two souls
That freely meet, and have no need
Of proving anything.

PAULA REINGOLD

I feel that we truly are free to be ... you and me. That we have no need of proving anything to each other.

Trying too hard and promising too much are never good for love. They make it a demanding emotion instead of the giving feeling that it is meant to be.

I don't expect you to love everything about me. And I don't have any desire to change you.

Of course, neither one of us is perfect—especially me. But wouldn't it be dull if we were? What would we ever find to fight about? And if we never had a fight, think of all the fun we'd miss, making up again.

I do want to be the best me I possibly can be for you. But always the real me. And I want you to always be you.

If we changed too much, it would be two different people ... not us ... in love.

Love needs new leaves every summer of life, as much as an elm tree, and new branches to grow broader and wider, and new flowers to cover the ground.

HARRIET BEECHER STOWE

Does it sound as if I'm about to contradict myself? I'm not. What I said about not trying to change each other, not trying to prove anything, still goes.

But growth is another thing. Love, like a tree, is a living thing. And it has to grow, put out new branches, if it is to keep on living.

Let's grow together—I know we will. Just finding out more and more about your feelings and needs, and vice versa. And let's keep ourselves open to new people, new ideas, new ways of sharing a better, more fulfilling life.

Our love will grow, too. Maybe it won't always hold the same kind of electricity and excitement that it does now. It will be even better in a different way.

Amy Lowell experienced this growth of love and she speaks of it in a beautiful way.

"When you came you were like red wine and honey,
And the taste of you burnt my mouth with its sweetness.
Now you are like morning bread,
Smooth and pleasant.
I hardly taste you at all, for I know your savor;
But I am completely nourished."

Love one human being purely and warmly, and you will love all. The heart in this heaven, like the sun in its course, sees nothing from the dewdrop to the ocean, but a mirror which it brightens, and warms, and fills.

It must be impossible to be in love with someone and not suddenly feel that love reaching out in so many different kinds of ways to everything and everyone around you.

That's the way it has been for me. Just as all the world loves a lover, a lover, just naturally, begins to love all the world.

I feel so much closer now to my family and my friends. They seem to think that I'm a lot more lovable, too. You really do bring out the best in me.

These days I even enjoy things I used to hate. Like getting up in the morning. Doing those "odd jobs" I kept putting off Mondays.

Ice cream cones are better than ever. So are bike rides and amusement parks and balloons.

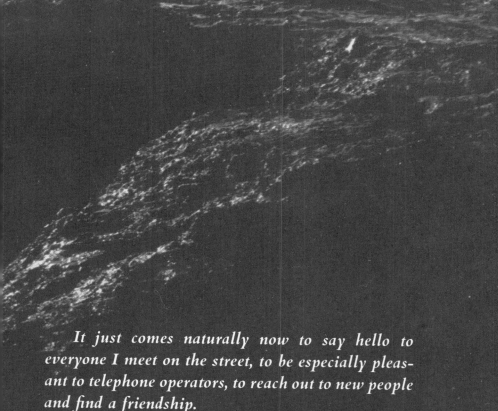

It just comes naturally now to say hello to everyone I meet on the street, to be especially pleasant to telephone operators, to reach out to new people and find a friendship.

I've even patched up a few old-standing quarrels that have kept me away from people I care about for too long. There's no room in me for grudges anymore.

I'm too full, full up to the top and overflowing, with love.

Love must have wings to fly away from love, and to fly back again.

EDWIN ARLINGTON ROBINSON

It would be so easy for me to promise you that I will love you forever. Mainly because I believe I will.

The thought of your promising me forever sounds tempting, too, but there are other things I want more ...

Give me yourself, but not all of yourself. Save a little just for you. And I'll save a little of me just for me.

Take time away from me, to be with friends, to be alone. And give me the same kind of freedom.

Leave spaces in our togetherness, times when we can stand back and look at the wonderful gift we share, times for missing each other. That sweet kind of sadness can add so much to the life of our love.

Don't ever feel trapped, obligated or, worst of all, bored.

Be absolutely sure of me—almost. Love needs challenge, a little bit of tension. It needs to be a see-saw with a delicate balance.

Want to want to be with me. Not because you have to. Not because of some oath, some paper, some law. Not because that's what I want. But because that's what you want.

Love me, today, with all your heart.

I want us both to have wings, to fly away from love, and to fly back again.

I love you now, today, as I have never loved anyone before you.

I believe, freely and joyfully, that I will always feel this way ... that I will have the rest of my lifetime to find all the words to tell you how much you really mean to me ...

to show you that ...

I love you because . . .

Photo Credits

Four By Five, Inc.—Cover, p.4, p.5, p.13, p.22, p.28, p.37, p.42, p.43; Michael Powers—end-papers; Gene Ruestmann—p.10, p.11; Jay Johnson—p.14; Lois M. Bowen—p.17; Frank Skully—p.20, p.21; Stanford Burns—p.27; Joan Walton—p.30, p.31, p.38, p.39; Courtesy of the state of Vermont—p.33.

Acknowledgments

The editor and the publisher have made every effort to trace the ownership of all copyrighted material and to secure permission from copyright holders of such material. In the event of any question arising as to the use of any material the publisher and editor, while expressing regret for inadvertent error, will be pleased to make the necessary corrections in future printings. Thanks are due to the following authors, publishers, publications and agents for permission to use the material indicated.

HOUGHTON MIFFLIN COMPANY, for "A Decade" from *The Complete Poetical Works of Amy Lowell.*

ALFRED A. KNOPF, INC., for excerpt from *The Prophet* by Kahlil Gibran, copyright 1923 by Kahlil Gibran, renewal 1951 by Administrators of C.T.A. of Kahlil Gibran Estate, and Mary G. Gibran.

LITTLE, BROWN AND COMPANY, for selection from *The Complete Poems of Emily Dickinson.*

RANDOM HOUSE, INC., for "Together" from *Embrace: Selected Love Poems* by Paul Engle, copyright © 1969 by Paul Engle.

Written by Dean Walley

*Set in Bembo roman and italic.
Designed by Sallie Baldwin and
Spencer Drate.*